¡VIVA LATINA!

Wisdom from Remarkable Women to Inspire and Empower

SANDRA VELASQUEZ

ROCK
POINT

First published in 2024 by Rock Point,
an imprint of The Quarto Group,
142 West 36th Street, 4th Floor,
New York, NY 10018, USA
(212) 779-4972 www.Quarto.com

Rock Point titles are also available at discount
for retail, wholesale, promotional, and bulk
purchase. For details, contact the Special Sales
Manager by email at specialsales@quarto.com or
by mail at The Quarto Group, Attn: Special Sales
Manager, 100 Cummings Center Suite 265D,
Beverly, MA 01915 USA.

10 9 8 7 6 5 4 3 2 1

ISBN: 978-1-57715-438-9

Digital edition published in 2024
eISBN: 978-0-76038-987-4

Library of Congress Cataloging-in-Publication
Data

Names: Velasquez, Sandra Lilia, author.
Title: !Viva Latina! : wisdom from remarkable
women to inspire and empower
 / Sandra Velasquez.
Description: New York : Rock Point, 2024. |
Summary: "Viva Latina is a
  powerful anthology of quotes from Latina
women to inspire at every stage
  of life"-- Provided by publisher.
Identifiers: LCCN 2024010113 (print) | LCCN
2024010114 (ebook) | ISBN
  9781577154389 (hardcover) | ISBN
9780760389874 (ebook)
Subjects: LCSH: Hispanic American women--
Quotations.
Classification: LCC E184.S75 V39 2024 (print) |
LCC E184.S75 (ebook) |
  DDC 081.082--dc23/eng/20240323
LC record available at https://lccn.loc.
gov/2024010113
LC ebook record available at https://lccn.loc.
gov/2024010114

Group Publisher: Rage Kindelsperger
Editorial Director: Erin Canning
Creative Director: Laura Drew
Managing Editor: Cara Donaldson
Editors: Keyla Pizarro-Hernández and Katelynn
Abraham
Cover and Interior Design: Amelia LeBarron
Illustration: Lucia Diaz 19, 25, 37, 43, 57, 63, 75,
81, 93, 99, 111, 117, 129, 135, 147, 153

Printed in China

This book is dedicated to all the women inside and outside of this book who are building a new world through their courageous choices. May we continue to be each other's mirrors and pillars of strength while making the world a more equitable place.

CONTENTS

INTRODUCTION

In a world that often underestimates and overlooks the vibrant and diverse voices of Latinas, *¡Viva Latina!* is a rallying call, an invitation to embrace the boundless power of Latina wisdom. This book is a celebration of the experiences that are inherent within our community. It aims to ignite the flames of bravery and joy, while fostering a deep sense of sisterhood and comradery among Latinas everywhere.

We have walked a unique path, shaped by the vibrant cultures and ancestral heritage that flow through our veins. From the fiery spirits of the Mayans and Aztecs to the passionate energy of the Caribbean and the indomitable strength of their ancestors, Latinas carry within them a legacy of determination and unwavering faith. *¡Viva Latina!* seeks to tap into this deep well of wisdom, untapped potential, and contagious joy, empowering Latinas to embrace their heritage unapologetically and courageously.

This book is not just a collection of stories or a mere guidebook. It is a living testament to the triumphs and challenges Latinas face every day as they navigate their identities, reclaim their narratives, and forge their paths. The pages within contain intimate stories, empowering reflections, transformative advice, and traditions, all carefully curated to spark courage and joy.

Throughout these pages, you will encounter Latina voices from various backgrounds, professions, and walks of life, who generously share their wisdom, hopes, dreams, and fears. From trailblazing artists and entrepreneurs to groundbreaking activists and educators, these extraordinary women will captivate your heart and inspire you to embrace your own unique journey. They are you; you are them. Their stories illuminate the path forward, reminding you that your worth is not determined by external validation but by your own self-belief.

This book encourages Latinas to reclaim their narratives, challenge stereotypes, and defy expectations. It serves as a guiding light for those navigating the complexities of cultural identity, gender norms, and societal pressures. It invites readers to embrace their cultural heritage while forging their own paths, reminding them that their voices matter, their stories deserve to be heard, and their worth is nonnegotiable.

Beyond individual empowerment, this book fosters a sense of sisterhood and community among Latinas. It serves as a reminder that we are not alone in our journeys. We are part of a vivacious tapestry of mujeres, united by shared experiences, challenges, and triumphs. Through the power of storytelling, *¡Viva Latina!* creates a space for us to connect, support, and uplift one another, fostering a community that celebrates and amplifies our collective strength.

As you embark on this transformative journey, prepare to be immersed in the vibrant colors of Latina culture. Together, we will embrace our roots, rise above adversity, and dance to the rhythm of our own beating hearts.

Let this be a beacon of hope, a celebration of Latinas' indomitable spirit, and an invitation to join a community of brave and joyful women. May these pages inspire you to stand tall, embrace your worth, and unlock the untapped potential within. The time has come for Latinas to rise, thrive, and shape a future that is unapologetically ours.

I have broken down the book into eight chapters that can be read in any order. Each chapter highlights a theme dedicated to encapsulating the amazingness of the women portrayed in it and guiding your journey of sisterhood. The categories are *Creer* (Believe), *Construir* (Build), *Explorar* (Explore), *Inspirar* (Inspire), *Amor Propio* (Self-Love), *Resiliencia* (Resilience), *Dirigir* (Lead), and

Familia (Family). Flip through when you need some wisdom or inspiration, or read in order; there's no wrong way of going about it. Find your favorite quotes and bookmark them for future use.

After reading this book, I hope that you are inspired to create the life you want—that you keep leading, building, inspiring, loving, and exploring as you trailblaze your way forward. Never give up and know that you are not alone. Life is not perfect, but there is always a way. I truly hope you find connection and hope here, as I have, in connecting with these women and reading their stories. May this also serve as a reminder to never forget your roots and where you come from. Instead, celebrate them so that the next generation of Latinas can be inspired by you.

Bienvenidas, hermanas. Welcome to a journey of self-discovery, empowerment, and sisterhood. Let us embark on this adventure together, as we stand in our worth, illuminate the world, and leave an indelible mark on history.

CREER

※

BELIEVE

"EL RECURSO MÁS IMPORTANTE ERES TÚ."

"YOUR GREATEST ASSET IS YOU."

In the depths of our souls lies an unwavering belief, a flame of resilience that fuels our pursuit of greatness. This chapter, aptly titled Creer, or Believe, serves as a profound reminder of the power that resides within us all. It is a call to harness that power, embrace our dreams, and cultivate an unapologetic belief in our own abilities.

Belief is the cornerstone of living out our full potential and our journey toward self-empowerment. Throughout history, Latinas have defied societal limitations, shattered glass ceilings, and left an indelible mark on countless industries and communities. Their stories serve as testaments to the transformative power that comes from believing in ourselves.

Within the pages of this chapter, you will encounter the stories of Latinas who dared to dream and refused to let anything hinder their aspirations. These women, from various walks of life and fields of expertise, will inspire you to embrace your own dreams, no matter how seemingly audacious. Through their narratives we will explore the common thread of determination and resilience that have propelled Latinas to greatness.

We learn that belief is not just a passive state of mind; it is an active choice. In the way you choose what to eat and wear every day, you can also choose to believe in your potential every single day. In fact, it is a must.

It requires courage and vulnerability to trust in our own capabilities and to silence the inner critic that tells us we are not enough or that we are delusional for wanting to accomplish our dreams. It takes resilience to embrace the possibility of failure as an essential part of growth. It is not easy. Belief demands that we step out of our comfort zones and defy the limitations imposed upon us, both by society and ourselves.

Self-belief equals confidence, and confidence is a magnet. People want to be near those who know where they are going. Belief is contagious. As Latinas, when we believe in ourselves, we inspire those around us to do the same. This chapter invites you to be a beacon of light for others, to uplift and empower your sisters, and to create a ripple effect within our communities. By standing in our worth and embracing our dreams, we become catalysts for collective transformation.

As you embark on this chapter, I invite you on a journey of self-discovery and courage. Together, let us believe in ourselves and in each other. The time has come to step into our greatness.

"From a very young age
I learned that believing in
a cause that is bigger than me
is fuel. Sometimes, believing
in your life's purpose,
that things at the end will work
out in your favor, is the only
thing you have, and it can be a
powerful space to embrace."

FANNY GRANDE
CEO OF AVENIDA PRODUCTIONS

F anny Grande is a Venezuelan American award-winning filmmaker with more than twenty years of industry experience. Born in the United States, she grew up in Venezuela where she began performing at a very young age.

When she moved back to the United States to pursue an acting career, she found that roles available for Latines were few and perpetuated negative stereotypes. Fanny decided her mission was to transform the image of the Latine community in the media. In college, she started making films that celebrated Latine contribution in the United States.

Fanny has received many awards and recognitions for her work, both in front of and behind the camera. She was one of eight fellows selected by Geena Davis for the See It, Be It Fellowship. She also served as the vice chair of Nosotros, the oldest Latine nonprofit in the entertainment industry. Recently, she completed the Stanford LBAN's business accelerator program.

In 2016, she cofounded an independent production company called Avenida Productions with her husband Nelson Grande. Committed to ensuring access to Hollywood for underrepresented communities, the company has raised more than $5 million for 225 projects that celebrate diversity. Avenida is about to launch the first large-scale streaming platform catering to Latine consumers in the United States.

"One way of being true to yourself is to always do your best work in every project, and if possible, doing more than what is expected of you. You never know who you can impress and what doors you may open by always giving the best of yourself."

MELY MARTÍNEZ
MEXICAN FOOD BLOGGER AND COOKBOOK AUTHOR

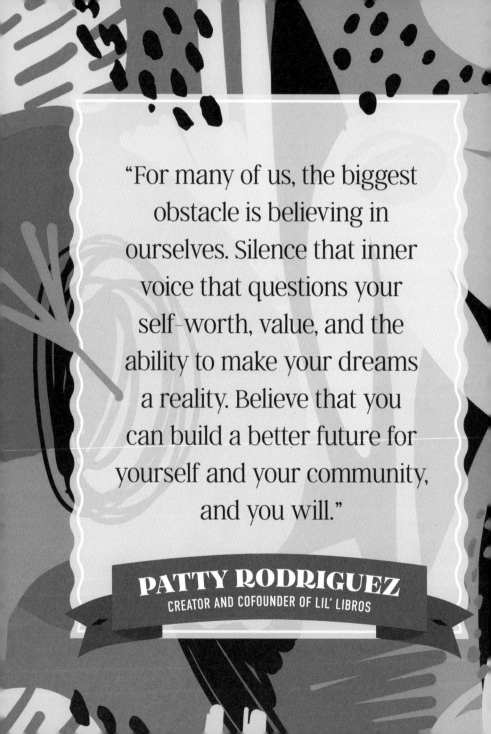

"For many of us, the biggest obstacle is believing in ourselves. Silence that inner voice that questions your self-worth, value, and the ability to make your dreams a reality. Believe that you can build a better future for yourself and your community, and you will."

PATTY RODRIGUEZ
CREATOR AND COFOUNDER OF LIL' LIBROS

19

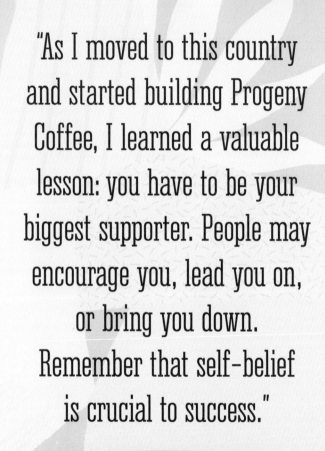

"As I moved to this country and started building Progeny Coffee, I learned a valuable lesson: you have to be your biggest supporter. People may encourage you, lead you on, or bring you down. Remember that self-belief is crucial to success."

MARIA PALACIO
CEO OF PROGENY COFFEE

Maria Palacio is a visionary fifth-generation Colombian coffee farmer with an unwavering passion for empowering her community. Born and raised in a celebrated coffee region of Colombia, she spent several years in New York City working in design before her heart led her back to her hometown in 2016.

After witnessing the struggles of her loved ones who made their living through coffee farming, Maria knew she had to take action. She cofounded Progeny Coffee with a fierce commitment to uplift others. Maria overcame numerous small business obstacles and cocreated a thriving distribution platform that empowers coffee farmers and helps lift them out of poverty. Her mission centers around the belief that education and entrepreneurship are vital to the success of these communities.

Her innovative approach and dedication have been recognized on numerous esteemed lists, including the *Forbes* Next 1000, *Inc. Magazine*'s 100 Female Founders of 2020, Mujeres Imparables by Telemundo, and *SFA*'s 12 under 35: Breakout Talent to Watch. Maria's inspiring story is also featured in the award-winning book *The New Latina: 100 Millennials Shaping Our World.*

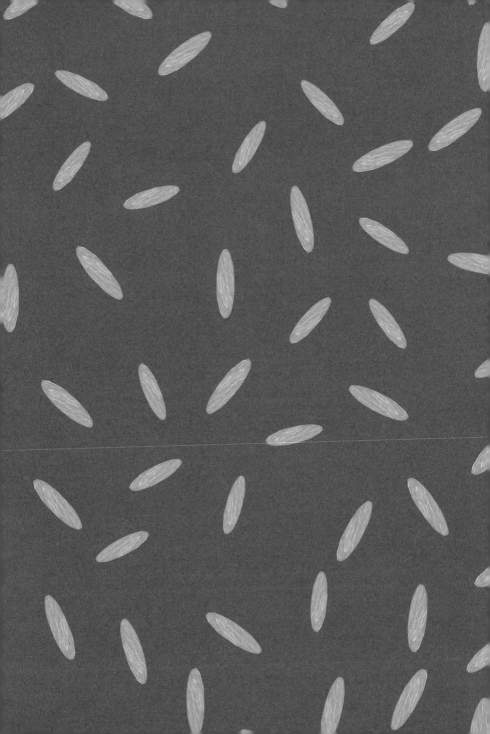

"Believe that you are worthy of a wonderful life today. Not in the future when 'the stars align' or when you achieve your audacious goals. You deserve creativity, joy, and recognition right now, especially when everything around you feels incomplete."

PAULETTE PIÑERO
FOUNDER AND CEO OF UNSTOPPABLE LATINA

"Everything you see manifested for someone else that inspired your heart is a clue for what can be true for you. The first step in believing is simply to believe in the spark, which is undeniable, given that you felt it. As you move toward your inspiration, witness your belief grow."

LINDA GARCIA
CEO OF IN LUZ WE TRUST

THE SPARK THAT LIT THE WAY

Belief begins with one person just as a flame starts with one spark. From that one spark, light is born. It can inspire and catch on to anything that stands near or bears witness to its shine. In Spanish, *luminaria* means "illumination." Luminaria traditions trace back to December 1590. Historically, the community would light up a street by placing paper lanterns along the sides of the road, forming a pathway of light. Today, many luminaria traditions are found in Latin culture, most often integrated as a part of celebrations of Winter Solstice, Christmas Eve, and religious ceremonies. But the main event is not the final illumination of the path; it is the process of one light blooming with the next following, and then the next. The light brings the community together for a night of beautiful alignment, that all starts with one flame.

CONSTRUIR

❀

BUILD

"ESCRIBE UNA NUEVA REALIDAD."

"WRITE A NEW REALITY."

I n our lives, we are both the weavers and the architects, shaping our own destinies with every choice we make and action we take. This chapter invites Latinas to step into their power, embrace their unique strengths, and construct the lives they envision. It is a call to action, a reminder that we have the ability to build a future that reflects our worth, aspirations, and dreams.

Building requires intentionality and a deep understanding of our authentic selves. As Latinas, we navigate the complexities of our cultural heritage, societal expectations, and personal aspirations. This chapter serves as a guide for the tools, insights, and wisdom necessary to build a life that aligns with our values and desires.

Within the pages of this chapter, you will encounter stories of Latinas who have fearlessly taken charge of their lives, building a foundation of success and fulfillment. These women, from diverse backgrounds and experiences, will inspire you to tap into your inherent strengths, harness your passion, and cultivate a sense of purpose that guides your every endeavor.

As you immerse yourself in the narratives within this chapter, you will witness the construction of an architect who designs vibrant spaces that celebrate Latina culture, weaving together history, tradition, and innovation. You will witness the creation of a writer who crafts stories that amplify the voices of Latinas, building bridges of understanding and connection. And you will witness the transformation of a community leader who builds networks of support and empowerment, constructing a stronger, more resilient sisterhood.

Building is not a solitary endeavor. It requires collaboration, support, and a network of allies who uplift and empower us. Throughout this chapter, you will find practical guidance on cultivating relationships, building networks, and finding mentors who can guide you on your journey. We will explore the power of community and the importance of fostering sisterhood, recognizing that together we can construct a world that celebrates and amplifies our worth.

Latinas have a long history of weathering storms, overcoming challenges, and rising above adversity. We are builders of resilience, drawing strength from our cultural heritage, familial bonds, and unwavering determination to write our own stories. The stories in this chapter are meant to give you insights on navigating setbacks, bouncing back from failures, and developing a resilient mindset to propel you forward.

In addition to personal growth, building extends to the realm of societal change. As Latinas, we have a responsibility to use our skills, talents, and influence to construct a more equitable and inclusive world. This chapter explores the importance of advocacy, activism, and using our voices to dismantle barriers and foster positive change. It invites you to become an agent of transformation.

As you embark on this chapter, I invite you to build alongside us and begin to lay the foundation of the life you envision. If you don't write your story, someone else will.

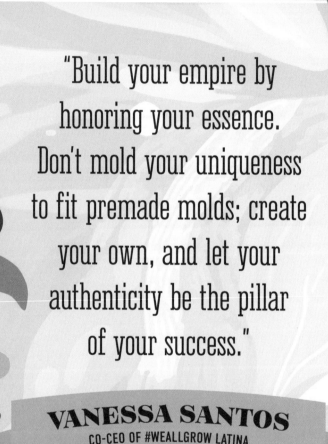

"Build your empire by honoring your essence. Don't mold your uniqueness to fit premade molds; create your own, and let your authenticity be the pillar of your success."

VANESSA SANTOS
CO-CEO OF #WEALLGROW LATINA

Vanessa Santos is an acclaimed entrepreneur, a motivational speaker driven by the heart, and a visionary executive leader. She proudly serves as the co-CEO and partner of #WeAllGrow Latina, a community dedicated to elevating and catalyzing transformative socioeconomic shifts in Latine communities.

#WeAllGrow Latina is more than a community; it's a testament to unity, bringing together Latinas and femme-Latines who wholeheartedly uplift one another. Guided by inclusivity, this space nurtures connection, ignites inspiration, and fuels collective growth. Vanessa's tireless dedication has garnered her prestigious accolades, including recognition by *Forbes* as a keynote speaker for their Most Powerful Women and the inaugural Impulsa Awards presented by Nationwide and the Hispanic Heritage Foundation.

While Vanessa's career boasts of remarkable achievements, her true passion lies in creating opportunities and nurturing spaces where Latinas and femme-Latines can flourish. Guided by her spiritual compass, she ardently addresses gender equality, leadership, wealth creation, mental well-being, and community empowerment. By infusing soul-centered spirituality into her work, Vanessa cultivates a transformative environment, empowering individuals to unlock their boundless potential. With authenticity, she is building a legacy that honors her unique calling and inspires others to do the same.

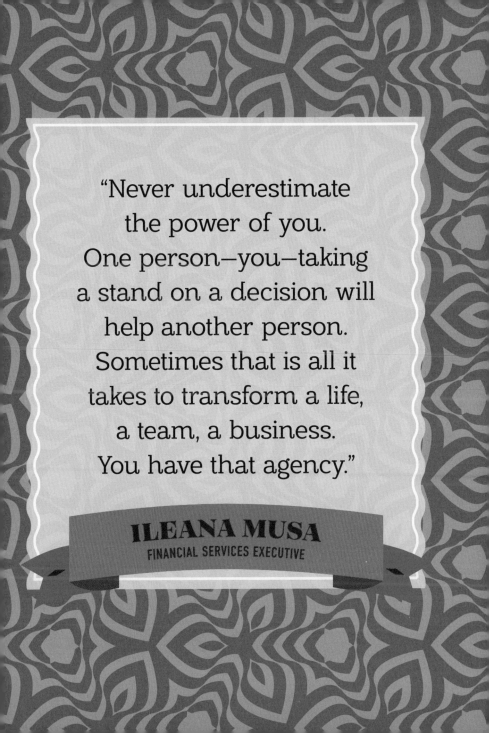

"Never underestimate
the power of you.
One person—you—taking
a stand on a decision will
help another person.
Sometimes that is all it
takes to transform a life,
a team, a business.
You have that agency."

ILEANA MUSA
FINANCIAL SERVICES EXECUTIVE

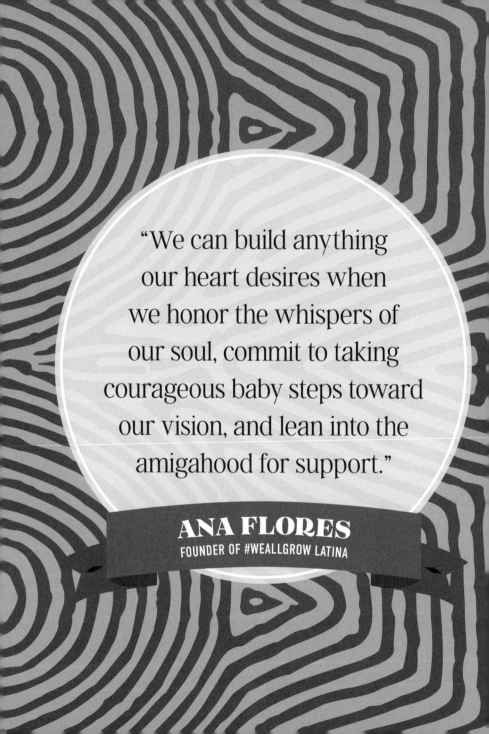

"We can build anything our heart desires when we honor the whispers of our soul, commit to taking courageous baby steps toward our vision, and lean into the amigahood for support."

ANA FLORES
FOUNDER OF #WEALLGROW LATINA

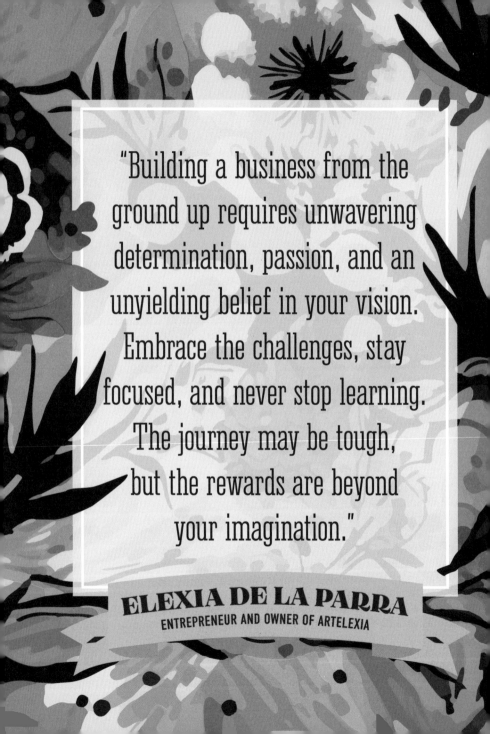

"Building a business from the ground up requires unwavering determination, passion, and an unyielding belief in your vision. Embrace the challenges, stay focused, and never stop learning. The journey may be tough, but the rewards are beyond your imagination."

ELEXIA DE LA PARRA
ENTREPRENEUR AND OWNER OF ARTELEXIA

Elexia de la Parra is a true testament to the power of determination and hard work as she fearlessly built her businesses from the ground up.

Starting with a humble farmers market stand, Elexia's entrepreneurial journey led her to create Artelexia, a beloved gift shop of Mexican art and handicrafts that has captured the hearts of many. With her passion for her culture and a keen eye for unique products, today, Artelexia stands as a testament to Elexia's unwavering dedication and her ability to build something extraordinary from scratch.

Not one to rest on her laurels, Elexia expanded her brand with Casa y Cocina, a haven for tabletop and gourmet products. The success of Casa y Cocina identifies and caters to the needs of her community, providing them with a curated selection of exquisite and high-quality items.

Elexia's entrepreneurial spirit continues to propel her forward as she works on her third venture, Cositas. With a laser focus on building a wholesale brand, Elexia is determined to bring the beauty of Mexican craftsmanship to a wider audience. Her commitment to excellence is the driving force behind her continued success.

Through her inspiring journey, Elexia de la Parra has proven that with a clear vision, relentless dedication, and a strong work ethic, one can build a successful business. Her story serves as a shining example for aspiring entrepreneurs, showing them that dreams can be turned into reality with passion and perseverance.

"Don't limit how big you can build something. Chances are you're not thinking big enough. With every new level that you aspire to build to, be strategic about how and when you will grow and what you'll need to get there. Even the tallest staircases start from the ground up."

KAYLA CASTAÑEDA
CEO OF AGUA BONITA

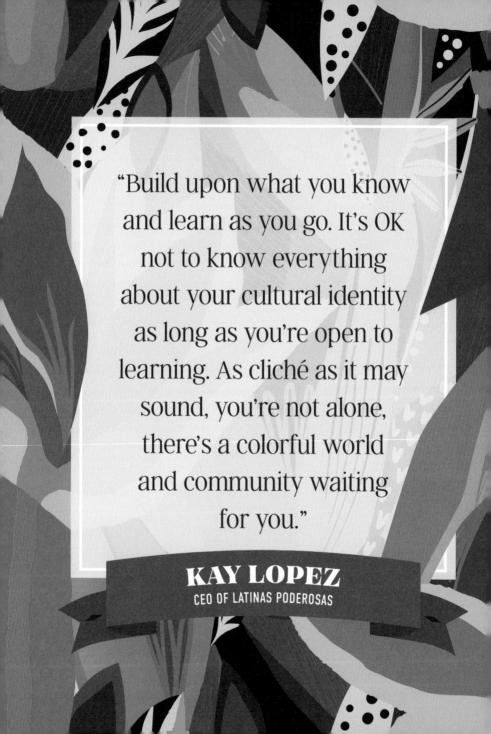

"Build upon what you know and learn as you go. It's OK not to know everything about your cultural identity as long as you're open to learning. As cliché as it may sound, you're not alone, there's a colorful world and community waiting for you."

KAY LOPEZ
CEO OF LATINAS PODEROSAS

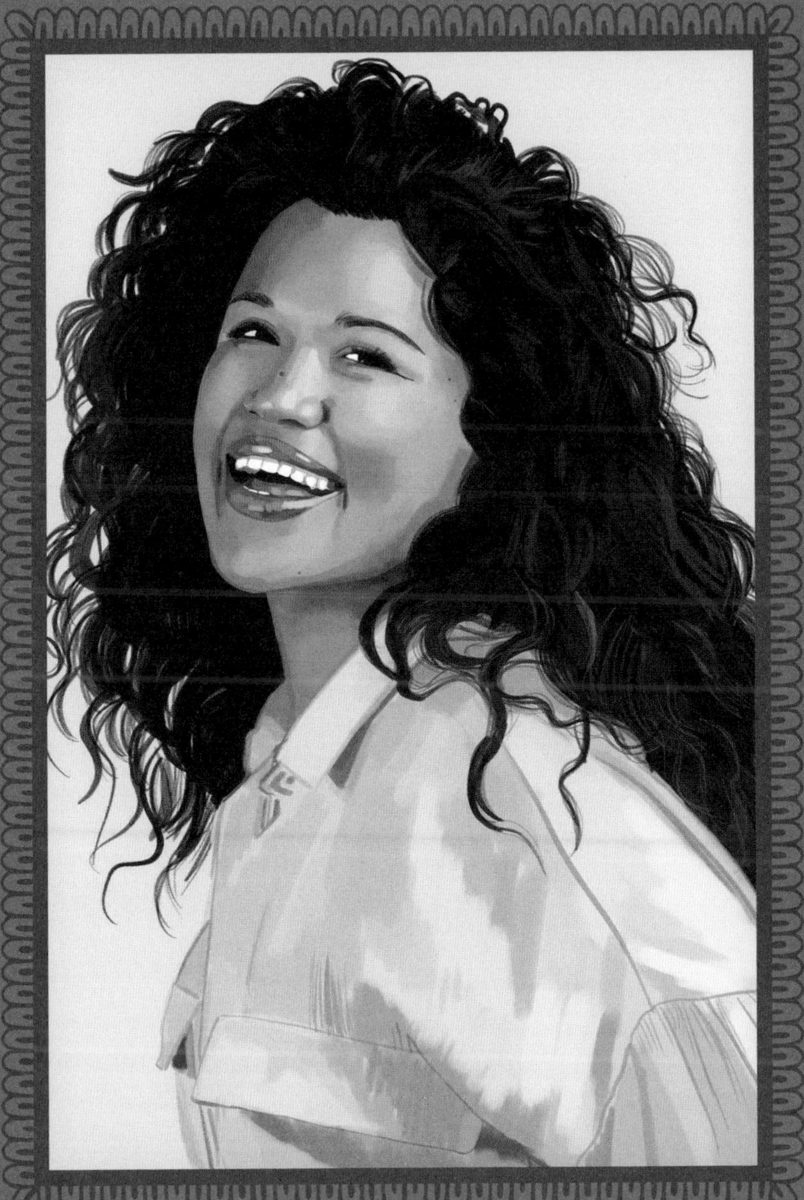

"Know what you bring to the table, use insights from your background as a competitive advantage, and think strategically about what you need to be successful. It takes perseverance to get where you're going, and the path is not always linear."

SASKIA SORROSA
CEO OF FRESH BELLIES

Saskia Sorrosa is originally from Guayaquil, Ecuador. She currently resides in New York with her husband and two daughters. She is the founder of Fresh Bellies, a savory snack brand that is turning pantries everywhere into an explosion of flavors.

Saskia was a 2023 JOURNEY Fellow with twenty-four other innovators tackling the most critical societal challenges. Prior to that, she was vice president of marketing for the NBA. During her tenure, she received several industry accolades for her innovation and leadership, including *Ad Age*'s 40 Under 40 and *Hispanic Lifestyle*'s Latina of Influence. She was named The Trendsetter in *Hispanic Executive*'s Top 10 Líderes.

As CEO of Fresh Bellies, Saskia has grown the company nationally since she founded it, gaining placements at major retail stores such as Whole Foods, Target, Walmart, Sprouts, and Kroger. The company won the Expo East NEXTY Award for Best New Natural Kid's Product and graduated from the Chobani Incubator. Fresh Bellies won first place at the NFL Players Association business accelerator. It was also selected as part of Goldman Sachs' Launch with GS Entrepreneur Cohort. Saskia has also had the opportunity to pitch it on *Shark Tank*.

FROM THE SEEDS OF TRADITION

Like a flower, you must tend to yourself to grow and build a path of your own. From planting the seeds to watering the roots, a flower requires collaboration and passion to bring it to full bloom. Flowers are as unique as they are vibrant, just like Latin culture. One of the most famous traditions of Medellin, Colombia, is the Flower Festival, or Feria de las Flores, which can be traced back to the nineteenth century. This tradition started as a local celebration to honor fruitful lands and the hardworking farmers who cultivated them. Today, it is a grand event that drives tourism and includes many artistic displays of various flowers and cultural traditions. Not only does this longstanding tradition acknowledge the agriculture of Colombian lands, but it is also one of Colombia's most important cultural events.

EXPLORAR

EXPLORE

"SIEMPRE PUEDES CAMBIAR TU MENTALIDAD."

"YOU CAN ALWAYS CHANGE YOUR MIND."

E very single day is an opportunity for growth, discovery, and self-exploration. This chapter is a rallying call for you to venture beyond the boundaries of comfort and uncover the depths of your potential. I invite you to allow curiosity to be your compass with self-belief as your guide.

Exploration is a fundamental part of our human nature, and as Latinas we are uniquely positioned to navigate the intricate legacy of our identities. Rooted in diverse cultures, traditions, and histories, we possess a wealth of experiences waiting to be explored. This chapter celebrates the spirit of exploration, inviting Latinas to venture into the uncharted territories of their own hearts, minds, and passions.

It is easier to stay behind the barriers that surround us. Sometimes these barriers are imposed upon us by our families, childhood friends, or places of work. But some of these barriers could be created by us. Often, we grow to accept them and become nervous to explore outside their perimeter for fear of judgment or failure. The stories shared in this chapter highlight women from various backgrounds and walks of life whose aspirations were greater than their fears. Staying curious is the key to evolution. Never stop learning or asking questions.

Exploration is not limited to external journeys; it is also the exploration of our thoughts, emotions, and dreams. It can be daunting to uncover parts of you that you didn't know existed. But by the same token, it can also be liberating to refine your life's true purpose. This can only happen if you allow yourself to explore. Some of the best revelations come while we are exploring new paths.

We often navigate the delicate balance between embracing our heritage and carving out our identities. This chapter embraces the complexities of cultural exploration and invites you to celebrate your roots, while also having the freedom to define yourself on your own terms. You can stay connected to your roots and still build a new reality.

At its core, self-exploration is a sacred pilgrimage that guides us through the maze of our own complexities and illuminates the corridors of our hearts and minds. It grants us the freedom to rewrite our narrative, honoring the stories woven into our identities while fearlessly scripting new chapters of growth and transformation. It is a pivotal tool that enables us to navigate the labyrinth of life, arming us with wisdom that comes from deeply understanding ourselves.

This chapter invites you to uncover your own passions and purpose. If you've had an idea, it is for a reason. Trust it. Follow it. This chapter also explores the power of building bridges, cultivating diverse relationships, and embracing the wisdom that resides within our communities. It is through different perspectives and engaging in meaningful dialogue that we expand our horizons and deepen our understanding of the world around us.

"Always have a curious mind.
As a high achiever, we can often
believe success is knowing all,
but that is a fallacy as we will
never know everything.
Our superpower is the ability
to have an explorative mind,
one that takes information
openly and always takes an
opportunity to learn."

MELISSA GONZALEZ
CEO OF THE LIONESQUE GROUP

Melissa Gonzalez is an award-winning innovator and storyteller. Continually pushing the boundaries of experiential retail—as principal at MG2 and founder of The Lionesque Group, an MG2 studio—she works to pioneer the integration of physical environments and digital retail, helping brands such as Kizik, Nordstrom, and Victoria's Secret foster consumer engagement and affinity.

Melissa has produced more than two hundred brick-and-mortar experiences across the country for both fast growing direct to consumer and digital native brands, as well as established retailers looking to think differently. Her projects are dedicated to creating immersive moments in a way that drives ROI and helps clients convey compelling stories to their audiences.

A passionate mentor and strategist, she works hand in hand with clients to understand their greatest aspirations. An innovator at heart, she has been consistently recognized as one of the leading Women in Design and Top Retail Design Influencers of the Year.

She is also the author of *The Pop-up Paradigm: How Brands Build Human Connections in a Digital Age*. When she is not dreaming up innovative retail spaces, she can be found exploring unexpected places (including places ten thousand feet above ground while skydiving).

"When I consider the term explorer, I think of a personal journey of self-discovery and uncovering one's identity. Ignore the distractions and focus on exploring your inner child, your culture, and your true self. Take the time to truly understand who you are, be present, and embrace all aspects of yourself with love."

MADRE ROMI
IDENTITY COACH

"Heading into the unknown is a scary thrill! Venture toward the thick dark forest of your life's questions, find your passions, and ignite your curiosity, until one night you'll find a trail of wondrous stars and understand they are the very same stars you are made of."

XENIA RUBINOS
MUSICIAN

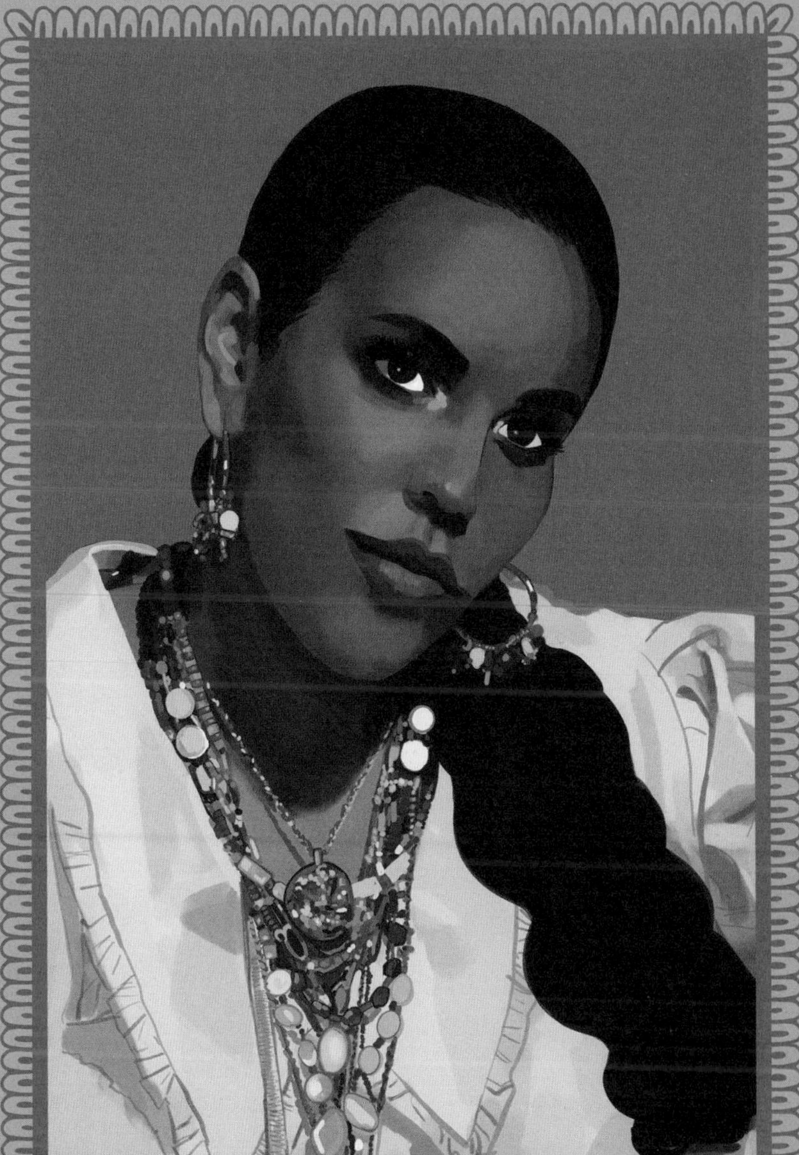

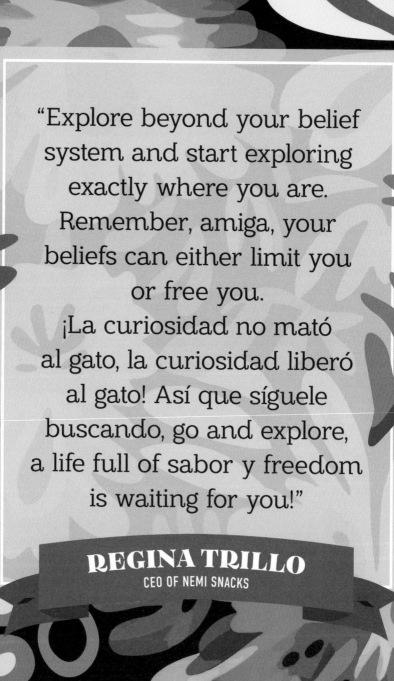

"Explore beyond your belief system and start exploring exactly where you are. Remember, amiga, your beliefs can either limit you or free you.
¡La curiosidad no mató al gato, la curiosidad liberó al gato! Así que síguele buscando, go and explore, a life full of sabor y freedom is waiting for you!"

REGINA TRILLO
CEO OF NEMI SNACKS

Regina Trillo is originally from Mexico City and is now based in Chicago. She felt unrepresented the moment she stepped foot in an American grocery store. At the time, she was pursuing her legal career as an attorney, focusing on immigration law and advocacy for human rights. But she wanted to start a business in the food industry.

Without any experience, Regina mistakenly felt incapable. And then she thought, if she could imagine a space with limitations and fear, why couldn't she flip that mindset and explore something different? Through her exploration, she learned that fear and limitations are only real until we make them unreal.

Nemi Snacks was founded with a mission to elevate the Latine community and Mexican cultura through better-for-you food with sombrero-free branding. *Nemi* means "to live" in the Aztec language. Inspired by her native Mexico, the brand makes fun and deliciosos crunchy sticks from seeds and nopales (prickly pear cactus) in Mexican-inspired flavors straight outta the cocina! Its mission is to satisfy more than a food craving.

Nemi works directly with farmers and mujeres holding leadership positions traditionally held by men. Regina is creating the business and community she wants to see, while lifting others along the way.

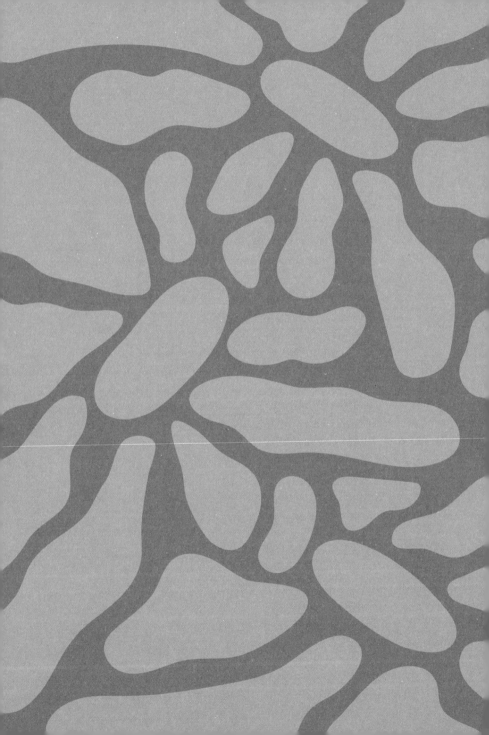

"As my dad would say, 'Con ámino, mija!' Lift those spirits, Mija! Our struggles are muy pesados but they have such beautiful potential to turn into something magical. And when they do, hold on to it tight. Porque siempre será tuyo!"

GABRIELLA CAMPOS
FOUNDER OF MIRADELA

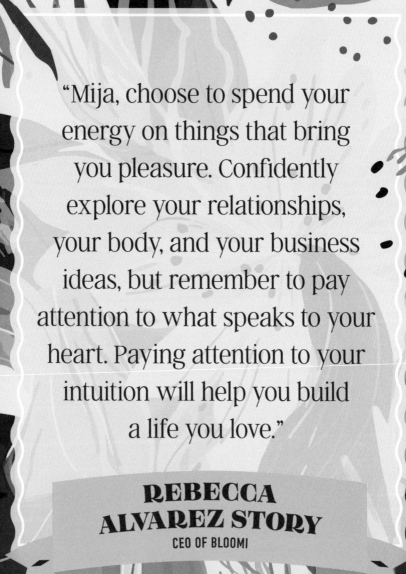

"Mija, choose to spend your energy on things that bring you pleasure. Confidently explore your relationships, your body, and your business ideas, but remember to pay attention to what speaks to your heart. Paying attention to your intuition will help you build a life you love."

REBECCA ALVAREZ STORY

CEO OF BLOOMI

A NEW DANCE TO LEARN

Self-exploration starts with taking something you know and making it your own. There is an inherent want to honor your culture and continue to celebrate and represent it throughout your life. But you cannot be afraid to add new elements and invent a new version of what has been passed down through generations. Ernestina Ramirez, founder of Ballet Hispanico, is an example of pushing the boundaries of Spanish dance styles by presenting them through a contemporary dance lens. She wanted to present modern Latin culture and show audiences that it was rich and more than the stereotypes that surrounded it. Ramirez shared her culture and amplified its voice so that it could reach even more people—so that it could inspire. Through exploration and pushing the boundaries, let your spirit and passions evolve your community into the future.

INSPIRAR

✺

INSPIRE

"PERMITE A TUS INSPIRACIONES CONVERTIRSE EN LOGROS."

"ALLOW YOUR INSPIRATIONS TO BECOME ACHIEVEMENTS."

Inspiration is the silent architect of change. It is an invisible spark that propels us to imagine a new reality, dream boldly, and act decisively in its pursuit. Many great things we enjoy today started as sparks in someone's imagination. Imagine if they hadn't courageously pursued them? Our world would be without art, music, or culinary recipes. What a boring world we would live in! We thrive on inspiration. It is a requirement for our evolution.

Inspiration is our ticket to freedom—an inner knowing that we can reimagine and improve our existing realities. We can create something new where a void once existed. The beauty is that it lives inside all of us in magnificent abundance. It knows no bounds. There is no age-, gender-, or country-based requirement to access it. Silently, it nudges us out of our comfort zones toward the greatest uncharted territory: growth. The only parameters are the ones we create or choose to believe are there.

At the heart of inspiration lies its transformative ability. It instills within us the courage to challenge stereotypes, break ceilings, and reshape narratives. It is one of our greatest innate powers. Often, we find ourselves attracted to those who have the courage to realize their inspirations. They are a testament to our own potential to do the same. We all have women in our lives who inspire us. But consider this: someone might be looking up to you too.

Our stories and journeys carry within them the power to touch hearts, shift perspectives, and spark change. This chapter celebrates the unique ability we possess to inspire and be inspired, weaving together narratives of resilience, passion, and triumph. Bear witness to the transformative power of inspiration through the experiences of Latinas who have blazed trails in their respective fields.

Inspiration extends beyond personal achievements; it encompasses the power of mentorship and tutelage. This chapter shows the significance of cultivating relationships that uplift and empower and the responsibility we carry to be role models for the younger generations.

Moreover, this chapter explores the transformative power of storytelling and the ability of our narratives to resonate deeply with others. Through our stories, we can inspire empathy, break down barriers, and create connections that transcend borders and cultures. By sharing our triumphs and vulnerabilities, we invite others to see their own potential and embark on journeys of self-discovery.

Be prepared to be both inspired and fueled to inspire others. Through insightful reflections and practical guidance, you will be equipped with the tools to harness the power of inspiration and create a ripple effect of empowerment and change.

I invite you to embrace the role of the inspirator: uplifting and empowering one another as we navigate the complexities of our lives. Let us recognize the profound impact we have on those around us and the world at large.

"Inspiration for me is believing in the fire inside yourself. No one can see it, but you can feel it. It's a deep desire to create things only imagined. Sometimes it burns brighter, sometimes it's a low flame, but it's always burning."

LESLIE VALDIVIA
COFOUNDER OF VIVE COSMETICS

L eslie Valdivia is the proud daughter of Mexican immigrants and farmworkers. The eldest of three daughters, she is a first-generation college graduate of Sacramento State where she received a bachelor's degree in communications with double minors in Spanish and journalism.

After graduating, Leslie worked as a communication and media relations professional in national and statewide public education campaigns. Through them, she has reached disadvantaged communities and communities of color to create social change and more equitable situations throughout California and the nation.

In 2017, Leslie became the cofounder of Vive Cosmetics, a beauty brand on a mission to create a more equitable beauty industry. They also wanted to build a foundation that authentically represented their community—their primas and amigas—starting from the founders all the way to the models and marketing campaigns. Since launching, Vive Cosmetics has been recognized by various national media outlets, including *O, The Oprah Magazine, Teen Vogue*, Buzzfeed, CNBC, HuffPost, and many more.

In 2019, Leslie was awarded the Latina Rising Estrella Award by the Sacramento Hispanic Chamber of Commerce for her contributions in business and the community.

"Today if you ask me what kind of inspiration I aspire to offer to others, it's the simple reminder to breathe. Every moment is loaded with endless opportunities for bliss; all you need to do is grant yourself permission to uncover them."

ANGEL AVILES
ACTRESS, COACH, AND AUTHOR

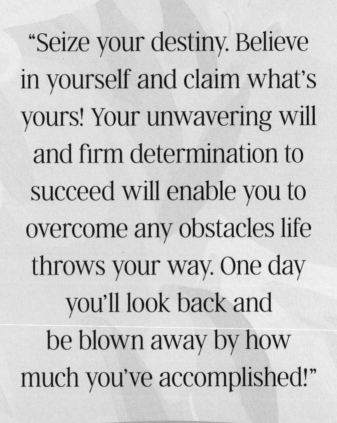

"Seize your destiny. Believe in yourself and claim what's yours! Your unwavering will and firm determination to succeed will enable you to overcome any obstacles life throws your way. One day you'll look back and be blown away by how much you've accomplished!"

EMILY PEREZ
FOUNDER OF LATINAS IN BEAUTY

"To inspire means to take action on an idea, passion, or dream. Inspiration is the oxygen of creativity. It can be sparked by any or all of the five senses or by a thought or memory. The beauty of inspiration is that you can find it all around you."

NAIBE REYNOSO
HOST OF *LATINAS TAKE THE LEAD* PODCAST

Naibe Reynoso is a multi-Emmy-winning journalist and author based in Los Angeles, California. She has contributed to various regional and international networks including CNN Espanol, Univision, REELZCHANNEL, and France 24.

Naibe was inspired to create her company, Con Todo Press, a children's book publisher that celebrates the joy of Latin culture, when she had a difficult time finding books for her own children that did the same. Con Todo Press amplifies the stories and voices of Latines and other underrepresented communities through colorful, award-winning, bilingual children's books. Naibe hopes to inspire future generations, so that they too can reach for their dreams.

Con Todo Press has been featured in the *Washington Post*, *Forbes*, BuzzFeed, *Los Angeles Times*, *School Library Journal*, and more.

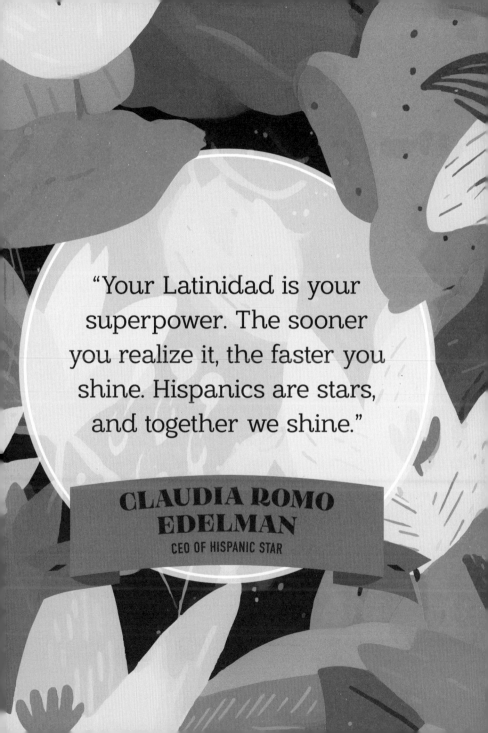

"Your Latinidad is your superpower. The sooner you realize it, the faster you shine. Hispanics are stars, and together we shine."

CLAUDIA ROMO EDELMAN

CEO OF HISPANIC STAR

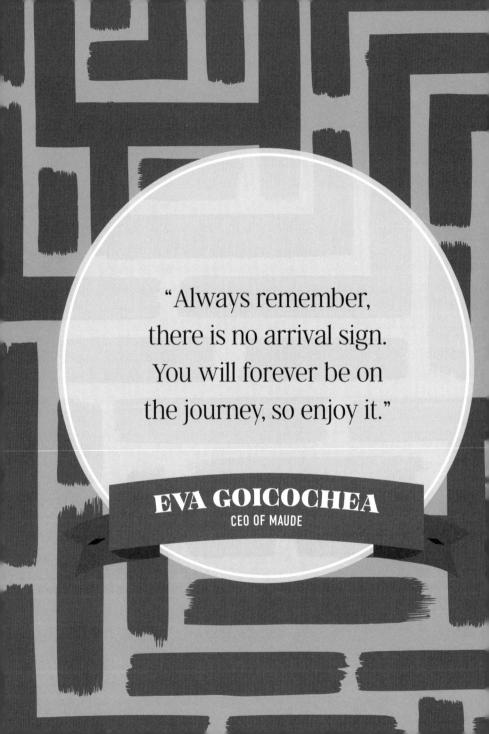

"Always remember,
there is no arrival sign.
You will forever be on
the journey, so enjoy it."

EVA GOICOCHEA
CEO OF MAUDE

A MOMENT IN THE SUN

Every new day begins with the rising sun. It crests the horizon, moving up into the sky until it shines down on us all to welcome a new beginning. The possibilities are endless for what you do next. In Peru, their biggest festival is the Inti Raymi, a nine-day celebration that pays homage to Inti, the sun god. It occurs shortly after the winter solstice, where the people coax the sun back. And inspired by the people, the sun makes its return. You can be inspired by anything in this world if only you allow yourself to begin again. Let your mind be coaxed to new ideas and be transformed just as the sun transforms back to its brightest form. Once you have found your inspiration, be inspired to shine that newfound light on your community, where you too can bring about a new beginning for someone else.

AMOR PROPIO

❋

SELF-LOVE

"LLENA PRIMERO TU PROPIO POZO."

"FILL YOUR OWN WELL FIRST."

L ove is a universal language that transcends borders, cultures, and time. It is a powerful force that has the capacity to heal, unite, and empower. Love starts with us. This chapter leans into the transformative power of self-love in the lives of Latinas. It celebrates the deep connections we cultivate and the healing it provides, as well as the collective love that binds us as a community.

Self-love is neither selfishness nor greed—quite the opposite. It is the commitment to treat ourselves as someone we love, so we may heal our own wounds, evolve, and, ultimately, love others unconditionally. Self-love is forgiveness. It is compassion. It grounds our spirit in the present (the only moment we can truly count on). To be frank, self-love is good for our health and longevity.

Over the course of history, women have been commended for their "selflessness" as a badge of integrity. Mothers have been applauded for their "sacrifices." I'd like to offer that, instead of viewing things as sacrifices, view them as priorities. This perspective gives us agency in life. It is intentional, instead of deductive. We have choices, and we can choose ourselves too.

Self-love is also rooted in the love we have for our heritage, our families, and our communities. It is a gift to love where we come from. This chapter serves as a reminder of the immense power that stems from loving our heritage. Let it serve as both a catalyst for personal growth and a driving force for change in the world around us.

Within the pages of this chapter, you will encounter stories of Latinas who have harnessed the power of self-love to transform their lives and the lives of those around them. These women will inspire you to embrace self-love as a guiding principle in your own journey. Through their narratives, we will explore the myriad ways in which self-love has served as a source of strength and a compass, as we shape the world around us.

Self-love is the recognition of our own inherent worth. This chapter explores the importance of cultivating a love for us—embracing our strengths and accepting our imperfections with compassion and grace. Self-love is what grounds us and fortifies us. It is the center from which we serve our communities and realize our dreams.

This chapter delves into the power of self-love as a unifying force. As Latinas we are bound together by a collective love for our culture, our heritage, and our shared experiences. It is through love that we build bridges, foster sisterhood, and create spaces of belonging. Together, let us embrace the power of self-love, fostering self-compassion, and cultivating a culture of empathy and acceptance. Let's start and end every day with love.

"If apathy stands as the antithesis of love, love has to be the driving force that propels you forward. Love of self, humanity, and the Divine. Accept that you must radiate the energy of that love, while expecting nothing in return. Consistently uncover your authentic self and confront the courage that love demands."

SHIRLEY RODRIGUEZ
ENTREPRENEUR

Shirley Rodriguez is a New York–based photographer, media producer, and entrepreneur. She is recognized for her visionary approach to media production with a keen eye for purpose-driven projects. She has built a distinguished track record in developing strategic campaigns for nonprofit organizations and government agencies, as well as companies seeking to make a positive impact on communities.

Over a decade ago, Shirley cofounded Create The Remarkable Inc., a full-service strategic creative studio dedicated to crafting video productions and campaigns for positive community impact. In addition to her role as a creative director, her photography has been featured in galleries and prominent publications, including *Latina, Crain's, Siempre Mujer, El Diario,* and *Vibe.* She has also produced campaigns for brands such as Olay, CoverGirl, and Fruit of the Loom.

Shirley's work goes beyond capturing compelling visuals; it reflects a personal mission to tell impactful stories, recruit support, fundraise, celebrate milestones, and shed light on important causes. Deeply rooted in the community, she has a background in grassroots organizing and teaching the arts. A proud mother of two, her children have been her greatest teachers, imparting valuable lessons about the true meaning of love.

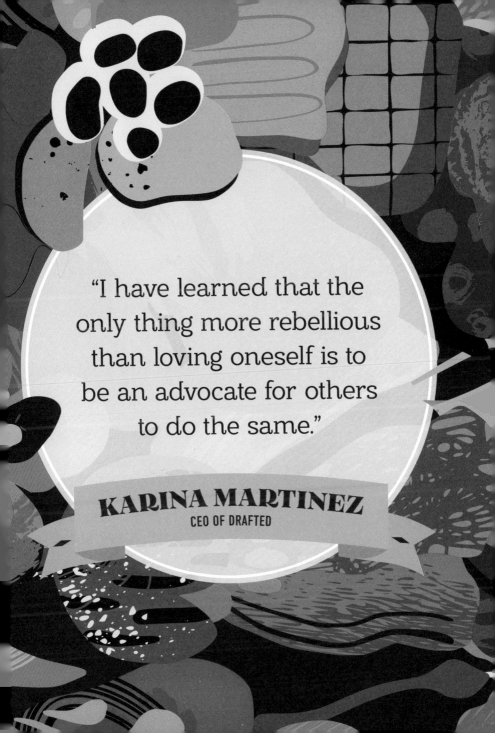

"I have learned that the only thing more rebellious than loving oneself is to be an advocate for others to do the same."

KARINA MARTINEZ
CEO OF DRAFTED

"Mi niña, this world is going to be rough and there's going to be a lot of challenges, but you know what? Everything is temporary. So, remember to always create from within, from a kind heart, and with intention."

JESSICA RESENDÍZ
CEO OF RAGGEDYTIFF

93

"There aren't any revolutionary words that I can say about self-love that haven't been said already. Revolutionary is the mujer, who despite her circumstances, and what the world is telling her, accepts herself as she is because she knows she is divina, worthy, and enough. To me, that is self-love."

ANABEL QUINTANILLA
CEO OF DE CHILLONA A CHINGONA

Anabel Quintanilla is known as a spiritual and emotional curandera for chingonas. For those who are ready to unf*ck their nervous system and align their cabeza, cuerpo, corazón y espíritu and gain clarity on their purpose. To stop doubting their potential and create the lifestyle that leads to peace of mind, conscious living, abundance, and self-love.

After decades of personal battles with weight, rock-bottom self-esteem, nonexistent self-love, and constant self-sabotage, Anabel decided to believe she was worthy of better.

In 2016, Anabel began her journey of forgiveness and healing and became a certified transformational coach. In her private practice, through her exclusive combination of neurolinguistic programming and transformational and spiritual coaching, she has helped countless women get to know, accept, and love their spiritual and physical selves more intimately.

Anabel believes that it is through this type of radical transformation, strength, and self-love that women can open doors to infinite possibilities.

"Everyone thinks love is about romance or passion. But love, at its core, is the comfort of being able to express every single emotion—good or bad—to yourself or someone else, knowing you'll be met with exactly what you need in that moment: support, acceptance, space, or tough love."

YESSY DOWNS
ENTREPRENEUR

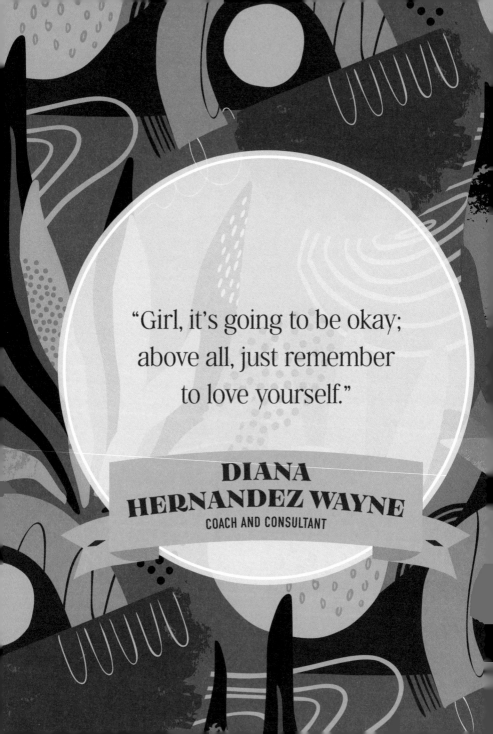

"Girl, it's going to be okay; above all, just remember to love yourself."

DIANA HERNANDEZ WAYNE
COACH AND CONSULTANT

THE SWEETEST INDULGENCE

Self-love should be defined in terms unique to the individual. Whether it's taking time for yourself, doing what you love, or celebrating your successes—no matter how big. With endless opportunities to embark on self-love, those with a sweet tooth might decide to visit the chocolate festival of Belize. Celebrated every year in late May, the event is held in the town of Punta Gorda, known as the chocolate capital of Belize. Over a three-day weekend, pay homage to the fruit that was once used as currency: cacao. While there, spoil yourself with the confections of local chocolatiers and artisan crafts. Whether you spend a day, an hour, or a minute for self-love, no excuse is needed when it comes to investing in our hearts and happiness.

RESILIENCIA

--- ✿ ---

RESILIENCE

"LA VALENTÍA
ES CONTAGIOSA.
LA RESILIENCIA
ES BELLEZA."

"COURAGE
IS CONTAGIOUS.
RESILIENCE
IS BEAUTY."

R esilience is defined in the dictionary as "the ability to withstand or recover quickly from difficulties." We often associate resilience with toughness or surviving repeated struggles. But resilience can also be self-empowerment. The power to choose your vision and desires over perceived failures or obstacles. The power to choose your self-worth over what others might think you deserve.

Resilience means choosing yourself over and over again.

A quiet strength, it enables us to bounce back from setbacks, disappointment, and heartache. We are not resilient for reward or applause, but simply because we know what we want and where we want to go. Resilience has the ability to transform pain into power and adversity into opportunity. It's not about avoiding difficulties but about navigating them with courage that refuses to be diminished.

The narratives of resilience among Latinas are as diverse as the hues of the Latin American diaspora. They unfold in the lives of mothers juggling multiple roles, young professionals breaking barriers in male-dominated fields, and elders who have weathered a lifetime of societal change.

In the richness of our cultural heritage, resilience is more than a survival instinct; it is an expression of our deepest values. It is the embodiment of the wisdom passed down from the abuela to the madre, a wisdom that teaches us to dance through life's challenges with grace, to find strength in our community, and to embrace our dual identities with pride.

The stories you will encounter in this chapter are not tales of stoic endurance but narratives of triumph over adversity. They echo the lived experiences of Latinas who have, time and again, stood firm in the face of hardship, drawing strength from their rich cultural histories. From the barrios to the boardrooms, resilience is the common thread that unites us all.

Resilience is not a quality reserved for the extraordinary; it is present in the everyday choices and actions of Latinas who persist in the face of challenges. Whether it is being overlooked in the workplace or being told to assimilate in schools, our resilience is the inner force that pulls us through.

In celebrating resilience, we acknowledge the strength inherent in the collective stories of Latinas. Let it be a rallying cry that echoes through generations, a reminder that within all of us lies an untapped reservoir of power waiting to be unleashed. Resilience is not about being unbreakable; it's about being able to bend without breaking, adapting to an inherently changing current of life while remaining rooted in one's authenticity.

As we explore the multifaceted nature of resilience, let us be inspired by the countless Latinas who embody this quality. Their stories are not monuments to unattainable perfection but testaments to the beautiful, messy, and transformative journey of standing in their worth. In their narratives we find the blueprint for our own strength and a reminder that resilience is not a destination but a continuous journey of self-discovery and empowerment.

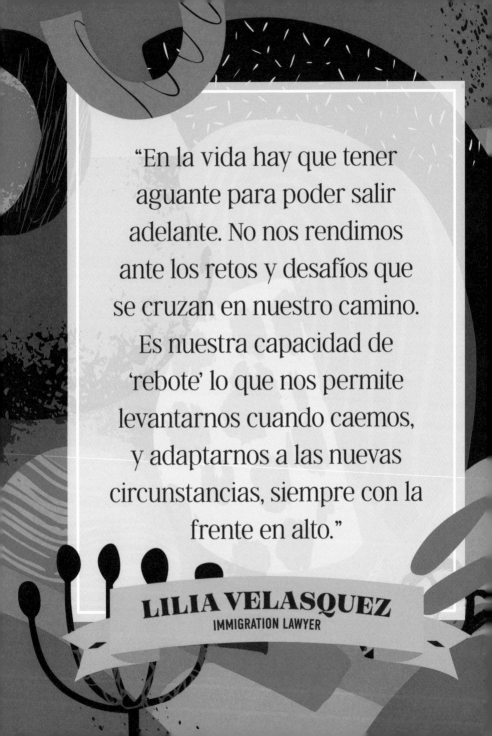

"En la vida hay que tener aguante para poder salir adelante. No nos rendimos ante los retos y desafíos que se cruzan en nuestro camino. Es nuestra capacidad de 'rebote' lo que nos permite levantarnos cuando caemos, y adaptarnos a las nuevas circunstancias, siempre con la frente en alto."

LILIA VELASQUEZ
IMMIGRATION LAWYER

Lilia Velasquez was born in a small Mexican village. At age nineteen, she immigrated to the United States with her mother and siblings.

Even though she could not speak English, Lilia enrolled in a community college. After a lot of effort, she graduated with an associate degree in secretarial science. Transferring to San Diego State University, she got her bachelor's in social work. During that time, she married Louis, a Mexican American law enforcement officer, and had a daughter named Sandra.

After college, Lilia enrolled at the California Western School of Law. In her last semester, she had a second daughter named Elena, and, against all odds, she passed the California Bar Examination on her first attempt. She went on to obtain her master's degree in international law and became a certified specialist in immigration law. For thirty years, she worked as an adjunct professor at her alma mater.

Lilia's practice today is focused on representing undocumented women who are victims of domestic violence or sexual abuse. She has received many awards and honors, including induction to the San Diego Women's Hall of Fame and El Premio Ohtli from Mexico. One of the most rewarding parts of her work is representing the vulnerable immigrant population.

"Take pride in your failures and the throes of your life, chiquita. Wear them loud and proud. Savor them. Find community in the process. It is because of these explorations—and, inevitably, mistakes—that you will live a fulfilled life and step into the power you know was meant for you."

LYANNE ALFARO
FOUNDER OF MONEDA MOVES

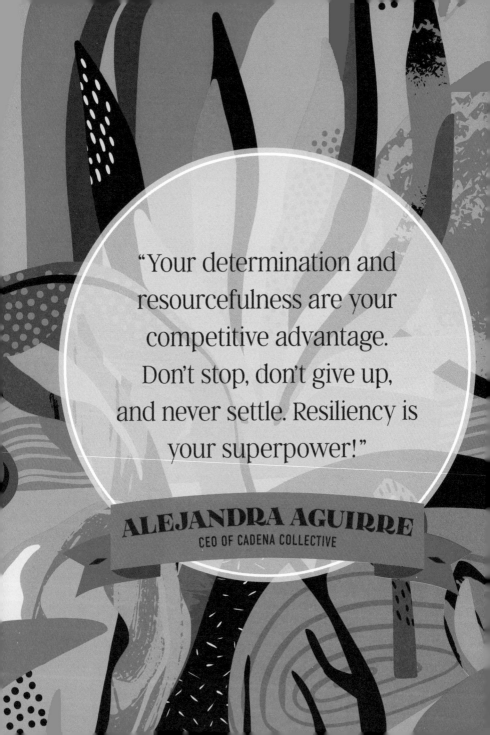

"Your determination and resourcefulness are your competitive advantage. Don't stop, don't give up, and never settle. Resiliency is your superpower!"

ALEJANDRA AGUIRRE
CEO OF CADENA COLLECTIVE

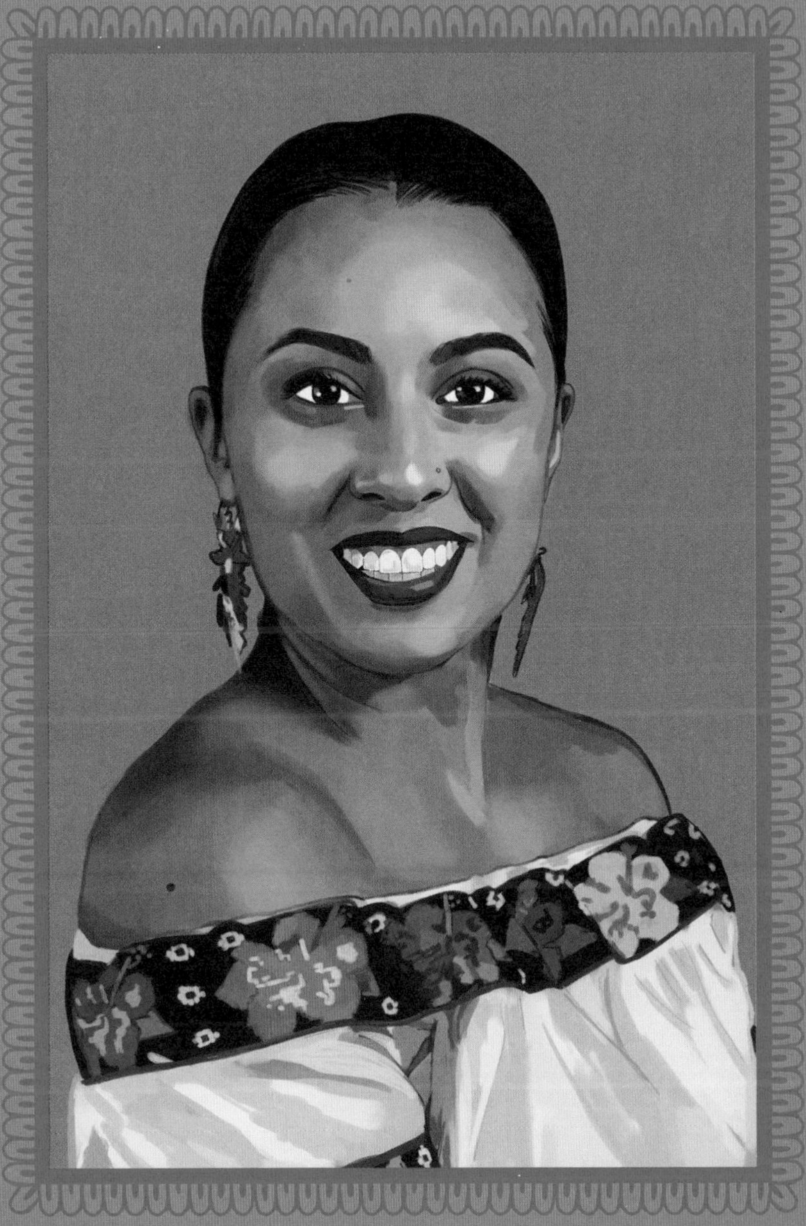

"In your toughest moments, remember that you represent something bigger: you're carrying not only your dreams, but also those of your community. Reflect on those who came before you and believed in all you could be. Draw strength from them and let their memory fuel you forward."

CORISSA HERNANDEZ
CEO OF NATIVO

Corissa Hernandez is a proud first-generation Mexican American who has defied odds and obstacles in her industries while always working to give back.

Corissa received her degrees from Cal Poly Pomona and UCLA. She worked as a Los Angeles public school teacher until the 2008 recession devastated her hardworking family. After seeing first-hand the need for adult financial literacy, she became a school teacher by day and a financial educator by night.

As her work blossomed, Hernandez cofounded Legacy Full Circle Financial & Insurance Services. There, she was further inspired to connect with people of color and underrepresented groups.

Soon, she opened three craft beer and cocktail businesses: The Empire Tavern, House of Xelas, and Nativo Highland Park. She created spaces where Latine voices felt seen, understood, and interconnected, while establishing herself as a standout female entrepreneur in another male-dominated industry. Despite the considerable challenges her businesses faced through the pandemic, she was devoted to her community to sustain operations.

Today, Corissa runs her businesses and gives back through positions on advisory boards and as a mentor. An "ambitious amiga," she's proud to have partnered and passed on her experiences to a hundred aspiring entrepreneurs of color.

"Loyalty over royalty. Our crown is not of gold but of trust and unity. In the empire of hearts, allegiance is our treasure, forging bonds richer than any throne could offer."

PERLA TAMEZ CASASNOVAS
FOUNDER OF LATINA EMPIRE

"Winds can rage, try to hold us back, and even knock us down. When our conviction for our vision, mission, and purpose are clear, nothing can stop us. We are the flagpole, not the flag. We will continue to stand strong and thrive, no matter the weather. We were built for storms."

BETH CARR
CEO OF FORTIFIED BRANDING

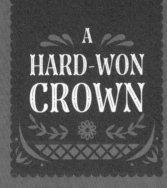

A HARD-WON CROWN

Resilience can come in many forms. We've seen the resilience of Latinas when pursuing a goal that is not easily within reach, triumphing even while others doubted them, and finding success when they themselves did not know they could have it. The spirit of Latin culture is laced with resilience, most notably showcased in the community on Easter Island, a special territory of Chile. During the annual event Tapati Rapa Nui, two groups compete for the title of the ruling clan of Tapati, with its main event being appointing the queen. The competition serves to share and preserve the ancestral traditions of the Rapanui people. It is comprised of tests of physical strength, ancestral knowledge, and skill and artistry. The inhabitants of the island get involved with pride and enthusiasm, welcoming any visitors to join in and experience the trials of their ancestors. Once all the excitement of the competition is finished, the winners enjoy a well-deserved parade and coronation.

DIRIGIR

❀

LEAD

"TU MISIÓN ES MÁS GRANDE QUE EL MIEDO."

"YOUR MISSION IS BIGGER THAN FEAR."

L eadership is the honor of being in service to others, working toward a mission greater than yourself. It is not solely about authority or power, though it can be viewed that way by some. Like most things, leadership is a mindset, a way of being that empowers us to navigate the complexities of life with confidence and purpose. This chapter celebrates the innate leadership qualities within Latinas and calls upon us to step into our roles as trailblazers, visionaries, and change-makers. A leader exists within you.

As Latinas, we possess a unique perspective shaped by our rich cultural legacy, our resilience in the face of adversity, and our unfaltering determination to create a better future. This chapter showcases the transformative power of leadership which can enhance Latinas' ability to make a difference, allowing them to lead with authenticity and compassion.

We have all witnessed the remarkable progress that unfolded just a generation ago within our families. Our parents may not have considered themselves leaders or trailblazers with their choices and actions perhaps being rooted in survival. Regardless of their drivers, their actions displayed courage—a tenet of leadership—which resulted in where we are today. I think of my own parents and what they have endured and navigated without playbooks, role models, or guarantees. And yet, here I am today, writing this book with our community for you. Who are my parents if not leaders? Undoubtedly, that is what they are. Yet, their actions were never fueled by a desire for applause or recognition. Their motivation was rooted in a commitment to greater progress and to contributing toward collective advancement. Imagine what future generations will look like if you step into your own power as a leader.

Leadership can be daunting because it exposes us to criticism, failure, and the responsibility of others who depend on our guidance. What if we fail? Self-doubt acts as kryptonite, weakening the potential for progress. The true power of leadership lies in its capacity to unlock human potential. It fosters a legacy of growth and enduring impact.

The stories within this chapter exemplify leadership through the experiences of Latinas who have made an impact in their communities and beyond. Moreover, this chapter explores the transformative power of self-leadership—the ability to navigate our lives with intention and purpose. Through self-leadership, we cultivate the inner strength and clarity necessary to make choices aligned with our values.

I invite you to embrace the power of leadership and to lead with truth and sympathy. Let us recognize the influence we have in shaping our own lives and the lives of those around us. It is our time to step into our full potential and lead.

"Embrace your unique story. Your bicultural heritage is not a barrier but your greatest strength. Lead with empathy, champion inclusivity, and never underestimate the power of opening doors for others. Your voice is a powerful tool for change— use it to uplift, inspire, and pave the way for the next generation of leaders."

BEATRIZ ACEVEDO
CEO OF SUMA WEALTH

Beatriz Acevedo is a proud Latina entrepreneur. As a child radio announcer in Mexico, she embarked on an entrepreneurial path in the United States and raised over $55 million for various ventures.

Beatriz is deeply committed to accelerating the success of the next generation of Latine leaders, with a focus on education, economic empowerment, and access to capital. At a White House conference for women of color, organized by First Lady Michelle Obama, she was asked to share her journey as an immigrant entrepreneur who grew up as a border girl between Tijuana and San Diego. After speaking, an audience member questioned how, as a Latina with an accent, did she manage to be a prosperous businesswoman. The question caught her by surprise.

Beatriz's immigrant background, accent, and pride in her culture have always been sources of confidence instead of obstacles. Being different has always been her superpower. Her unique identity and experiences are what make her a leader and that mindset has been integral to her success and ability to inspire others.

Her mission as a leader is to create legacies, nurture communities, and advocate for representation, all with the goal of making a lasting, positive impact on the world.

"Hermanas, your journey is a symphony of strength-defying odds and rewriting destinies. Embrace and stand tall in your roots and let the world witness the extraordinary tapestry you weave. Keep forging ahead. You are the architects of inspiration for generations to come."

AURORA ARCHER
CEO OF THE OPT-IN

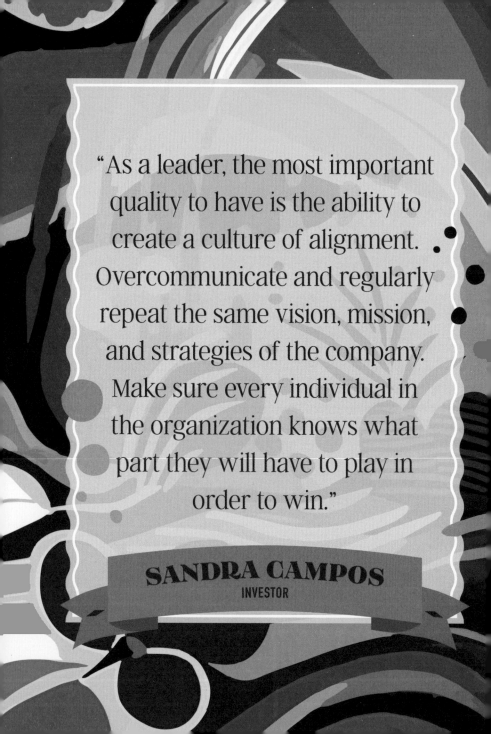

"As a leader, the most important quality to have is the ability to create a culture of alignment. Overcommunicate and regularly repeat the same vision, mission, and strategies of the company. Make sure every individual in the organization knows what part they will have to play in order to win."

SANDRA CAMPOS

INVESTOR

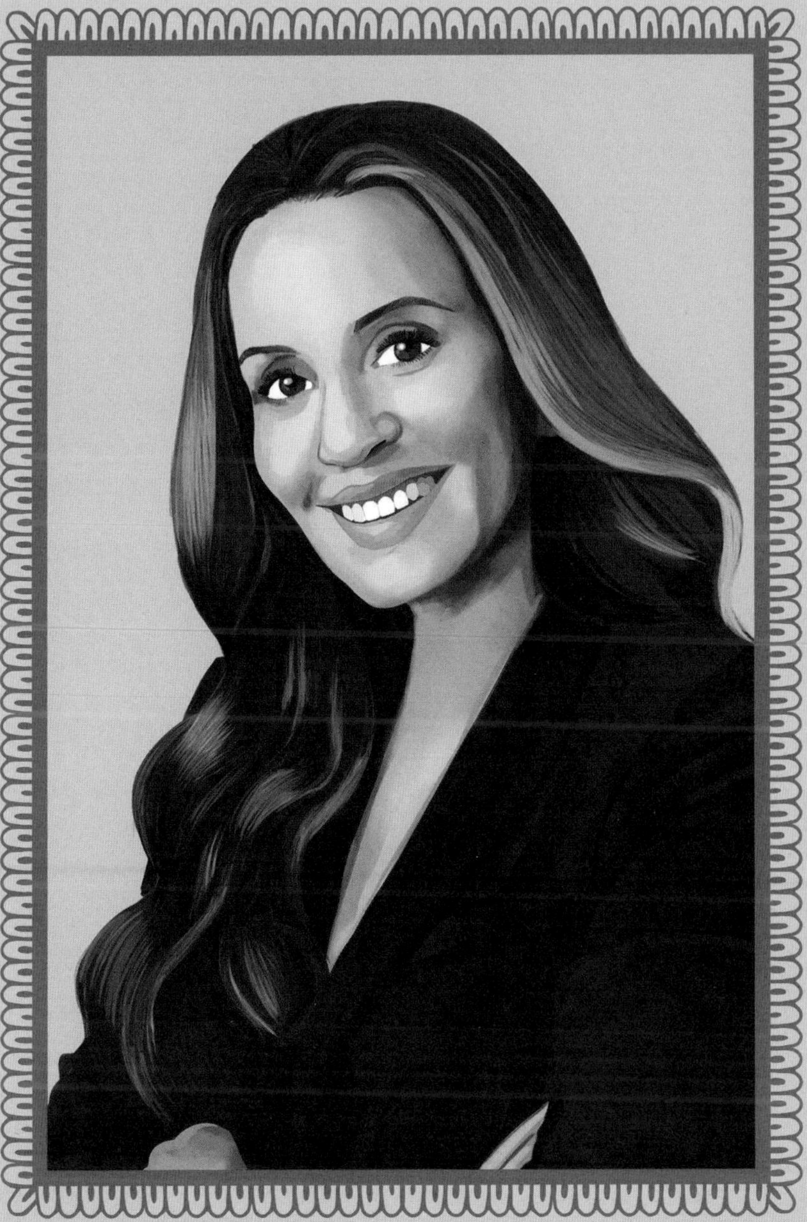

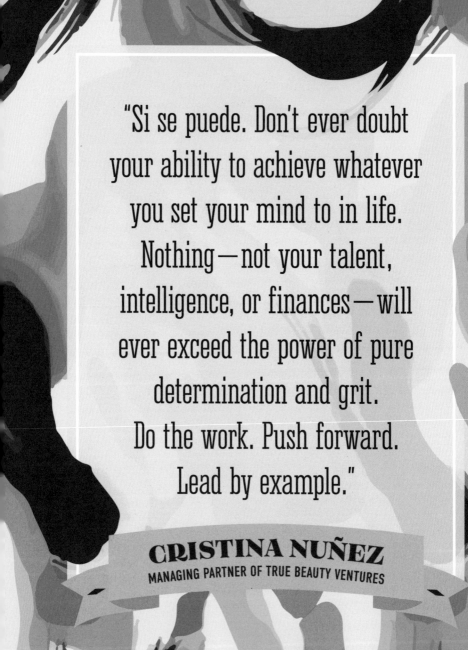

"Si se puede. Don't ever doubt your ability to achieve whatever you set your mind to in life. Nothing—not your talent, intelligence, or finances—will ever exceed the power of pure determination and grit. Do the work. Push forward. Lead by example."

CRISTINA NUÑEZ
MANAGING PARTNER OF TRUE BEAUTY VENTURES

Cristina Nuñez is the cofounder and General Partner of True Beauty Ventures. With seventeen years of investing and operating experience in the consumer industry, her focus recently has been on beauty and wellness.

Cristina graduated magna cum laude from Duke University. She spent half her career as an operator at brands such as Clark's Botanicals, Laura Geller Beauty, and Equinox. She started her professional career in finance as an associate at L Catterton and then as a senior associate at Tengram Capital Partners. She was also an analyst in the consumer and retail investment banking group at UBS.

Cristina cofounded True Beauty to bring true sector expertise to early-stage beauty investing. She sits on several boards, including maude, Youthforia, Crown Affair, caliray, Moon Juice, Cay Skin, and Feals. Her contributions to the industry have garnered strong recognition, including being named one of 2023's Most Inspirational Women Leaders by *WWD* and featured on *Latino Leaders*' 100 Latinas of 2023 list.

Cristina is a proud Cuban American living in Miami, where she was born and raised by Cuban immigrant parents. She strives to make an impact and drive change in an industry that has historically been underrepresented by people like her in leadership positions.

"Infuse your life with action. Don't wait for it to happen. Make it happen. Make your own future. Push the boundaries and believe in your ability to create impact through ambition, resilience, and honoring your rich heritage."

LAURA MORENO LUCAS

INVESTOR

"Your journey as a leader is an ecosystem of strength, vulnerability, and continual growth. Inspiring leaders give others the space to shine and value varied perspectives for personal growth. Embrace the challenge of listening and foster a culture where Black and Brown voices lead. Prove that we can do well while doing good."

YANIRA CASTRO
CEO OF HUMANITY COMMUNICATIONS COLLECTIVE

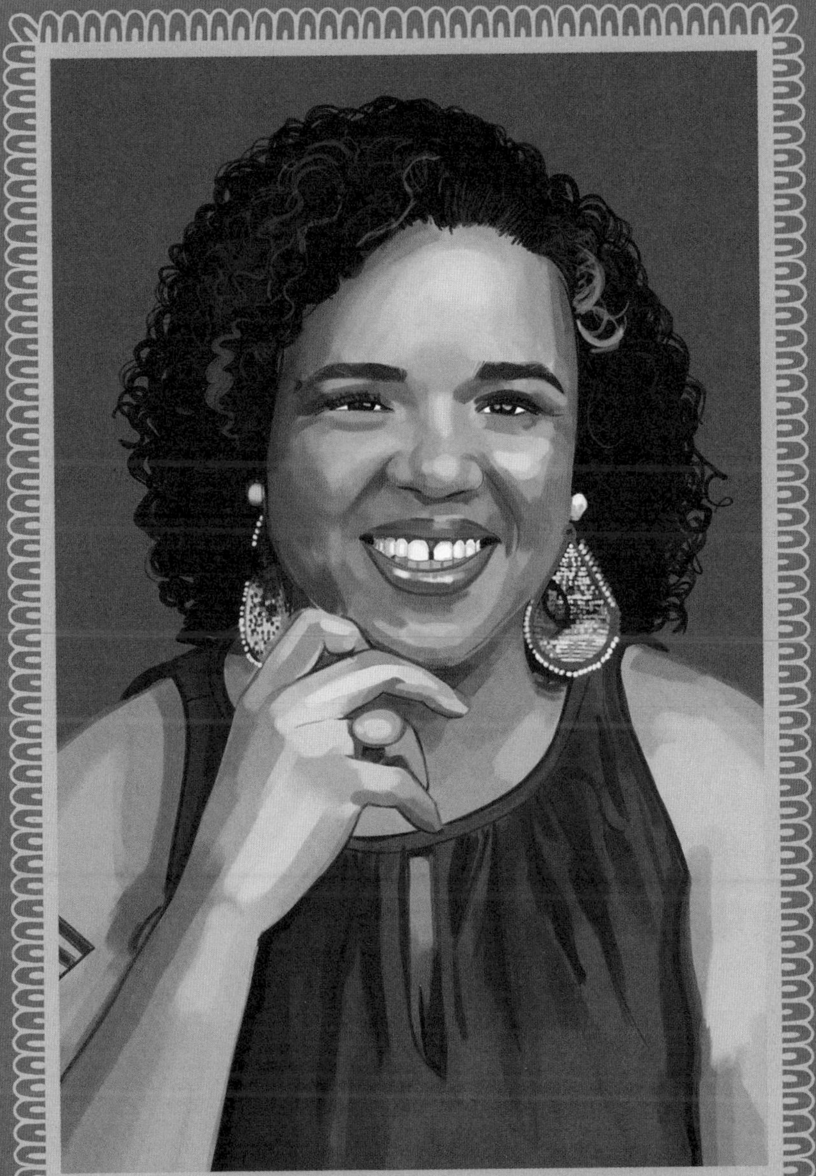

THE WORK UNSEEN

The independence of Mexico is a great achievement of the Latin community, but while Father Hidalgo is most often recognized as the leader of this feat, we cannot overlook the heroines of the story. Unknown to some, many women helped in the movement, from spying and manufacturing munitions to using their skirts to smuggle money, messages, and supplies to those who needed it. Mexican women were also known to seduce soldiers to join the cause and worked as soldaderas to feed, clothe, and nurse the sick and injured troops. And we cannot forget the brave women who dressed as men to fight, such as María Luisa Gamba, alias la Fernandita, or María Manuela Molina, la Barragana, who was granted the rank of captain after effectively leading a corps seventy strong. While the history of change-making women has long been swept under the rug and overshadowed by the celebrations of men, we are empowered knowing that there are great Latina leaders out there facing adversity and continuously proving just how powerful women can be.

FAMILIA

❀

FAMILY

"MI FAMILIA
CORRE A
TRAVÉS
DE MÍ."

"MY FAMILY RUNS
THROUGH ME."

Family is the cornerstone of our lives, the foundation upon which our identities, values, and sense of belonging are shaped. This chapter celebrates the profound impact of familial bonds in the lives of Latinas and explores the rich wisdom, strength, and love that emanates from our familial connections.

As Latinas, our families are the heart and anchor of our journeys. We are shaped by the stories, traditions, and legacies passed down through generations. Not only are we influenced by our families, but we have immense pride in them—their journeys, hardships, and successes. We are keenly aware of our ancestors who allowed us to stand where we stand today. This chapter champions the transformative power of family, inviting you to honor your roots while forging your own path.

As you read through this chapter, you will witness the power of family through the experiences of Latinas who have found solace, guidance, and inspiration within these sacred relationships. Family extends beyond traditional definitions, encompassing the broader Latine community and the connections we forge with those who share our experiences and values.

There is the family we are born into and the family we choose. We have the capacity to shape our own definitions of family, choosing to surround ourselves with individuals who uplift and support our life path. It is through these chosen families that we cultivate a sense of belonging and feel understood. Family becomes a mirror that reflects where we came from while also grounding us in the present.

Family bonds transcend time. Even when they are no longer with us, we feel the power of their spirit within. As Latinas, we feel a deep connection to our past and can use it as strength to build the future.

Humanity is just an intricate network of family ties that bind us together as a species. Everybody is someone's child, sibling, or parent. And all families across the globe share common stories of love and loss. In times of adversity, the strength of family shines brightest. It is a network of safety nets, catching us when we stumble and lifting us when we fall. Shared joys are amplified and burdens are lightened through the communal spirit. The family becomes a compass, pointing us toward our true north and guiding us through the labyrinth of life.

The power of family lies in its ability to provide a foundation of support during trials and triumphs. It is a refuge where laughter echoes and tears are understood, a space where vulnerability is not a weakness but a testament to trust. Within the family unit, lessons of compassion, empathy, and cooperation are learned, shaping individuals who become contributors to a collective legacy.

This chapter explores the significance of building and nurturing these communal bonds and creating spaces of love and belonging that transcend bloodlines. I invite you to think about the impact your family has had on your life—the good and the bad. We have the power to choose what to carry forward and what to leave behind.

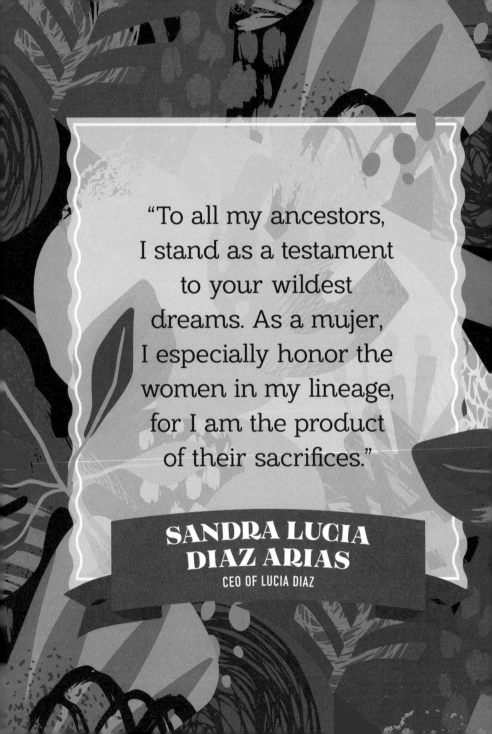

"To all my ancestors, I stand as a testament to your wildest dreams. As a mujer, I especially honor the women in my lineage, for I am the product of their sacrifices."

SANDRA LUCIA DIAZ ARIAS
CEO OF LUCIA DIAZ

Sandra Lucia Diaz Arias is the founder of Lucia Diaz, a Latina brand dedicated to the art of representation. Her mother, Luz Elena Arias Builes, who served as her first entrepreneurial inspiration, was renowned for her exceptional Colombian arepas.

Sandra's mother fiercely believed in her artistic abilities when others claimed she would end up being nothing but a starving artist. Powerfully, her mother would affirm, "Tú eres capaz." In other words, her mother told her to disregard those who lacked courage in their own lives.

Sandra's grandmother, Lucia, purchased Sandra's first commissioned piece as an artist—a self-portrait for Mother's Day. Lucia Diaz pays homage to her grandmother, whose dreams were left unfulfilled due to societal pressures on mujeres. Diaz desires to embody generational wisdom and carry the aspirations and dreams of her ancestors.

Strengthened by the resilient mujeres en su familia, Sandra Diaz has collaborated with esteemed brands, including Tiffany & Co., CHANEL, Carolina Herrera, and more. Soon, she will be addressing the United Nations.

"My father was always a legacy-minded person, and instilled that thinking in me. It's a great lesson because the most valuable gift we can leave our children and future generations is to help them understand how even from a young age, they can start making decisions that impact their own legacy."

ANGELA SUSTAITA-RUIZ

CHAIRWOMAN OF BRILLA MEDIA VENTURES

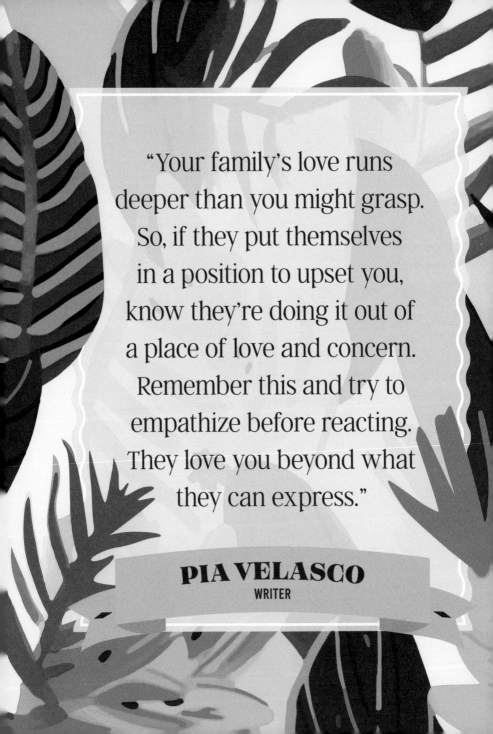

"Your family's love runs deeper than you might grasp. So, if they put themselves in a position to upset you, know they're doing it out of a place of love and concern. Remember this and try to empathize before reacting. They love you beyond what they can express."

PIA VELASCO
WRITER

"Everything I have accomplished and overcome is because of mis abuelas and their teachings. That guerrera spirit, that drive rooted in survival and strength: to be great, to be better! I strive to be that example and teach it to my children. Para mis chaparritas, las tengo siempre en mi alma."

CECELIA MEADOWS

CEO OF PRADOS BEAUTY

Cecelia Meadows is the founder and CEO of Prados Beauty. Prados is the first Xicana and Indigenous owned beauty brand in a mega retailer in the United States.

From a small town in Arizona, she is a proud Xicana and Indigena (Yoeme). The eldest in her family, her siblings provide her with much drive and success. Cecelia spent many summers on the traditional homelands of her Yoeme father and grandparents in Sonora, Mexico. Today, she shares the stories of her upbringing and teachings that were passed down to her to her children so that they will always have a connection to their land and culture.

Launched in 2019, Prados Beauty has gained recognition, including *Allure*'s Best of Beauty Awards 2022 for their eyeshadow pans, pots, and palettes. Prados was also a 2023 Impact Finalist for the BeautyMatter NEXT Awards.

Through cosmetics and storytelling, Cecelia has dedicated her brand to telling stories and representing Xicana/o and Indigenous peoples. Prados Beauty often collaborates with Native and Indigenous artists to tell stories through the packaging and designs. The products are on display in 610 Thirteen Lune stores within JCPennys across the United States. A portion of all profits from the Steven Paul Judd (Kiowa & Choctaw) collection are donated to Indigenous communities, veterans, and children with special needs.

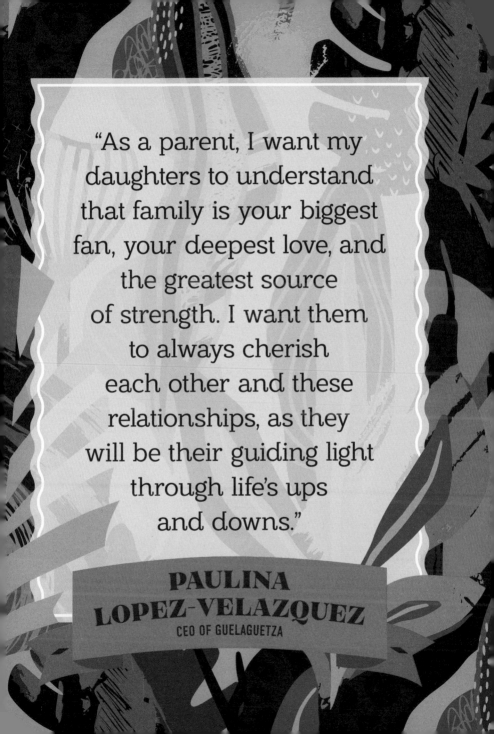

"As a parent, I want my daughters to understand that family is your biggest fan, your deepest love, and the greatest source of strength. I want them to always cherish each other and these relationships, as they will be their guiding light through life's ups and downs."

PAULINA LOPEZ-VELAZQUEZ

CEO OF GUELAGUETZA

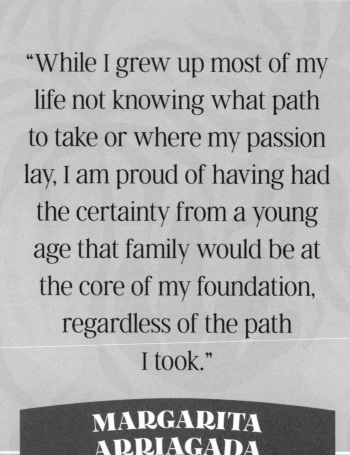

"While I grew up most of my life not knowing what path to take or where my passion lay, I am proud of having had the certainty from a young age that family would be at the core of my foundation, regardless of the path I took."

MARGARITA ARRIAGADA

CEO OF VALDÉ

"El lazo familiar es la fundación de nuestra cultura latina."

MABEL FRÍAS
CEO OF LUNA MAGIC

Mabel Frías is the daughter of immigrant Dominican parents. She is grateful to her grandmother, mother, and her childhood experiences for planting the seeds of valuing the hard work, positivity, and discipline needed to achieve one's dreams.

Mabel and her two siblings grew up in a botanica (healing store). As children, they watched their grandmother and mother operate the establishment as a means to offer spiritual guidance to the patrons and as a means to feed the family. These early memories of helping out in the family business led by strong women showed Mabel the power of positivity, resilience, humility, and collaboration. These aspects became the pillars that helped lay the foundation for building Luna Magic with her sister, Shaira.

One of the fondest memories she has from la botanica was listening to life mantras and wisdom from her Spanish-speaking grandmother at the register. One of her favorite lessons from her grandmother— which anchors how she sees the world today—is that no matter where life takes you, "hay que siempre tener los pies firmes sobre la tierra."

A CULTURE OF COMPLEXITIES

The full Latin community spans wide across the globe. From Mexico to Brazil and all the way across the ocean to Spain, the culture spans miles upon miles of land and history. With the added mixed heritages, the fabric expands into something truly unending. There are so many cultural expressions within this community that it is difficult to capture them all in their entirety. We can, however, witness just a portion through the Guelaguetza festival in Oaxaca, Mexico, also known as Los Lunes del Cerro or Mondays on the Hill. Celebrated in the month of July, representatives of the different regions of Oaxaca perform the dances of their region while wearing traditional clothing. It is a celebration meant to bring communities together and share what makes their heritage unique. For several hours, the city showcases each region through a presentation that boasts where they came from and what they bring to the Latin tapestry.

LIST OF CONTRIBUTORS

THANK YOU

First and foremost, I would like to express my deep gratitude to the warrior women who participated in this book. It is a privilege to be in your orbit and inspired by your courage every day.

My mother, La Flama de La Justicia, for leading by example what it means to #EmbodyTheBold.

To all the women who send me letters, emails, and DMs daily about how I inspire them, please know that it is not about me; it's about *us*. May we all collectively step into our full potential, write a new narrative, and stand in our worth, forever.

ABOUT THE AUTHOR

Sandra Velasquez is the Chicana founder of Nopalera, an award winning, culture forward, beauty brand rooted in Mexican heritage. Nopalera launched in the middle of the pandemic from Sandra's Brooklyn apartment without outside funding or savings, while she was working three jobs and raising her daughter. The brand is now sold nationwide, with Sandra making appearances on the *Today Show*, Univision, Telemundo, as well as *Shark Tank* Season 14 where she turned down two offers by standing in her worth.

Prior to launching Nopalera, Velasquez was the leader of the Latin Alternative band Pistolera, that toured internationally, opening for artists such as Los Lobos and Lila Downs, and had its music featured on hit TV shows such as *Breaking Bad* and *Sons of Anarchy*, and NPR's *Tiny Desk* concert series.

Sandra is the host of *The Nopalera Podcast* where she shares the journey of building Nopalera. She is passionate about equality and empowering women to live to their full potential.